D1521670

Front endpaper: photograph by Francesca Galliani.
Pages 46-47: photograph © by Nan Goldin: *Lynette and Donna, Marion's Restaurant, New York*, 1991. Courtesy Matthew Marks Gallery, New York.
Back endpaper: Sylvia Rivera, photograph by Val Shaff.

Text permissions: Tomas Medina
Photo Editor: Amy Steiner
Special thanks to Bonnie Eldon, Sandy Gilbert, Charles Miers, Tara Rodgers, Henry E. Scott, and Timothy Terhune.

First published in the United States of America in 1997 by
UNIVERSE PUBLISHING
A Division of Rizzoli International Publications, Inc.
300 Park Avenue South
New York, NY 10010

97 98 99 00/10 9 8 7 6 5 4 3 2 1

Library of Congress Catalog Card Number: 97-60138

Printed in Singapore

OUT FACTS

JUST ABOUT
EVERYTHING
YOU NEED TO KNOW
ABOUT GAY AND
LESBIAN LIFE

FROM
OUT MAGAZINE

EDITED BY
DAVID GROFF

DESIGNED BY
STEVE HIETT
WITH
LOSEFF RODGER GREY

UNIVERSE
PUBLISHING

T

E
N
T
S

When we opened the doors to *Out* Publishing's first office a little
more than five years ago, I didn't imagine we'd have such a fabulous handbook to mark our half decade's progress and to bring you
all the facts of out life as we know it. *Out* started in 1992 with a
mission to find the stories, pictures, and examples that reflect the
awesome energies, battles, passions, and achievements happening in
American gay and lesbian communities every day. And we continue
in that spirit. Whether reporting on challenges in Washington,
landmarks in the arts and entertainment in Hollywood, break-
throughs in AIDS research and treatment, or independent ways of
living our lives everywhere, *Out* holds up a mirror—sometimes
reflecting back amazing new realities, sometimes appraising difficult troubles—to the often unbelievable world around us.

TRO

And the best part is that people have and continue to respond. After nearly fifty issues, we have opened the doors to more readers than any gay or lesbian magazine in history. Our commitment is to quality and to providing our readers with an information source they can trust and rely upon for the full scope of their lives and concerns. Gathering ever more readers and respect should come along automatically if we keep those priorities in sight.

Out Facts takes you on a little slice of our journey to date and offers some pointers, reminders, and giggles along the way. It seems like everything is changing all the time in our lives as gay men and lesbians. So let us give you a few facts and clues. The rest is, as they say, history.   **Sarah Pettit**   Editor in Chief, *Out*

Whether you're a lipstick lesbian in Atlanta, a gayboy circuit partier in West Hollywood, a dedicated activist in D.C., an accountant in Los Angeles, or a Mississippi country dyke with her own farm and softball team, you can agree on one queer truth: We've come far fast. Every day, who we are and how we live grows more central to the American experience.

This decade may not always be the Gay '90s—we've had our share of setbacks and sobering circumstances, from the debacle of the military ban on lesbians and gay men to the not-quite inexorable advance of AIDS. But we have certainly grown more visible, more relaxed with our sexual identities, and sometimes even more willing to play with them. As we establish our own citizenship in America, we can't take for granted how much we accomplish just by saying, I'm gay, I'm a lesbian. The very act of being forthrightly homosexual remains a political, social, and personal accomplishment.

By the time of the 1993 March on Washington, when we assembled on the Mall, we extended to the horizon, having grown too vast, too vocal, and too varied to wear one set of labels. From poetry readings to rodeo roundups, from rock music to cyberspace, we are everywhere, doing everything. Along with our ever-changing outfits and attitudes, we've got myriad opinions about how we should live, how we should love, and what rights we should seek. For every five people who fight for lesbian and gay marriage you'll find two who think it's the worst thing that's happened to lesbian and gay people since mandatory showers after gym class. Some of us are drag queens, some of us are drag kings, and some of us find drag a big old bore. Views divide on Bill Clinton, gay Republicans, deep house music, tattoos, the gay ghetto, and the roles and conflicts of gay men and lesbians in the movement. But whether you're listening to disco or country, fighting for your rights or flexing your party muscles, you know that being lesbian or gay offers a multitude of options and interpretations.

The very nature of being out is changing so fast it can take your breath away. The military ban that galvanized gay politics was barely whispered as an issue before January 1993. The drive for lesbian and gay marriage didn't even show up on queer radar screens until 1994. Less than a decade ago, k.d. lang was singing in Canadian dance halls, RuPaul was living in Atlanta with his mother, there was no hope for an AIDS cure, the Speaker of the House did not have an out lesbian sister, gay and lesbian parents lived carefully in the shadows, cyberspace was not even a concept, hardly any corporations had anti-gay discrimination clauses (much less domestic partnership benefits), and America thought gay and lesbian marriage was a contradiction in terms.

Now, in a format compact enough to stick beneath your pillow, *Out Facts* is here to help you delight in those complications. With *Out Facts*, the people, events, and facts you first read about in *Out* magazine now comprise an up-to-date manual to smooth your way to being your best and most contemporary self. From your rights to your forebearers to how we live and love, as you choose your own scene and scheme for being lesbian or gay, *Out Facts* aims to inspire you to be an informed, entertained, engaged, artful, and happy homosexual.

So fasten your seatbelt and take a deep breath.

David Groff   Editor, *Out Facts*

WHO

ARE WE

it takes 1

I didn't always have a lot of use for gay radar. In the community where I came out, if I wanted to find someone of the homosexual persuasion, I simply pointed towards the nearest girl with a commie dyke slut button pinned to her sleeve.

It wasn't until I traveled to the Midwest in 1977 that I discovered queer bars with peepholes at the entrance and code words to gain entry. I met the world of married lesbians; women with a husband, 2.5 kids, and a serious lesbo affair going on behind the Donna Reed façade. Sure, some people will seek out the obvious appearances: lack of feminine clothing (the spinster schoolteacher who wears men's suits from J.C. Penney's), or noting her favorite jukebox oldie: "I Never Loved A Man (The Way I Love You)." It's easy to tell who the baby dykes are, with their homemade haircuts or the political babes with their work shirts and steel-toed boots. The butches can be spotted by a four-year-old, even if they aren't always so aware of it themselves.

Cherchez La Femme

Long before "sheer lipstick" and "lesbian chic" became synonymous in the national media, dyna-femmes were expertly drawing on their eyeliner and completing an eight-hour work-day in three-inch heels. Glamour dykes have functioned as some of our brightest Hollywood celebs and most notorious porn stars. How was anyone to know? Independence and a decent manicure are dead giveaways. Look for that gal who doesn't seem to be standing by, leaning on, or fawning over a man. Compulsory heterosexuality is not so much about women desiring men as it is about depending on them. Of course, lesbians do have a craving for soft curves and wet caresses, but it's just as much about living on our own terms as a W-O-M-A-N.

Everyone wants to be a dyke now; everyone craves our freedom, guts, and knowing looks. When I saw a paparazzi photo of Axl Rose wearing a "Nobody Knows I'm a Lesbian" T-shirt, I didn't waste two seconds thinking about him. I looked a little closer at the picture, because the woman who gave him that shirt must surely be in the background. Hey, did I say background? Pardon my disgusting pre-Lesbian Avenger consciousness lapse. I'm sure the dyke was the one snapping the shutter.

Susie Bright

to know

GAY

Using That Intuitive Sixth Sense

As a people, gay men are blessed with certain rare talents: the ability to think of Joan Collins as a currently exciting star; a flair for discovering new brands of underwear; and, best of all, *gaydar*—the art of spotting sisters, no matter how concealed, invisible, and straight-looking they are. Gaydar is an intuitive aptitude that surpasses anything in nature. A wildebeest couldn't spot another wildebeest with the same precision with which we can track down other

ILLUSTRATIONS: Mark Falls

GAYDAR

kindred spirits, whether in a mall, on a football field, in an army barracks, or even at home ("Daddy, what are you doing with Mommy's pendant?"). There's something in the walk, the talk, the pursing of the lips, the posing of the wrist, that tips us off with great certainty, even when they're holding a live grenade or sporting a wedding ring.

Gaydar doesn't only apply to stereotypical things, which just about anyone can pick up on. It's all too easy to spot a certain sashay, a

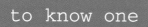
to know one

slight over-pomading of the hair, a devotion to grooming, floral arrangements, dance music, and T-shirts that virtually anyone with access to the Rainbow curriculum or a video of *The Boys in the Band* can detect. Many such things—bandannas, goatees, *Beverly Hills 90210* lunch boxes—are signifiers that we purposely use in order to be spotted, so it takes no supernatural skill to take note of them.

But piercing through the physical and emotional language of the closet cases and mystery folks is a whole other, more challenging game that requires a far subtler gaydar. That little exercise requires an uncanny sense that this man in straight drag in a straight setting selling you shoes at straight prices is actually, deep down, a girlfriend, even if he has one. Maybe it's the way he strikes up a conversation so readily, his noticeably campy sense of humor, his assumptions (how did he know you wanted the shoes for a night out at a dance club, and how did he know what that particular dance club was?), or his references (does any straight man know the names of all the *Designing Women* cast replacements?).

And there are other clues. Like the way people look back at you on the street when you cruise them. Straights are generally either titillated against their will or completely revolted, but other gays are scientific about it—they turn around and measure you up and down before letting their response show. It's the way a man expresses admiration for another man—you can tell from the inflections whether he simply thinks the guy is cool or whether he'd actually like to plow him. It's the way he tries on a lot of different outfits before settling on one, even if it's the same one he always settles on—a T-shirt, jeans, and backwards cap.

Or maybe it's something intangible that you pick up between the lines, between the signs—but, in any case, you just know.

Straights don't have gaydar, thank Mary. But *we* certainly do. We calculatedly add up every clue from head to toe and come up with a pretty firm guess—and oh what a sweet reward it is when you've got him in some unspeakable insouciant position on the bathroom floor and can finally inwardly smile, "I knew it!"   **Michael Musto**

SLEATER-KINNEY   **HAVE YOU HEARD?**

Sleater-Kinney is a powerhouse band. Their effect is raw and fresh, dissecting fear, alienation, and sickness with candor, vulnerability, and brute force. "A lot of my songs are about letting go of fear, or trying to," explains singer-guitarist Corin Tucker. "And a lot of people can relate to that in a lot of different ways."   **Ray Rogers**

PHOTO: Sue Schaffner

(Q)ueer

zɪn

A QUICK AND EASY GUIDE TO YOUR TRUE SEXUAL PREFERENCE

How do you know if you're a gay man or lesbian? Sometimes, as we all know, it's not as simple as biology. You're an eco-feminist Lesbian Avenger with a penchant for Karen Carpenter. You're a gym bunny who feels more comfortable in Birkenstocks after a session with the butt-blaster. An Armani-only woman who pats on Eau Sauvage after-shave. So what are you really? Try our version of 20 questions and find out your true "preference."

Donna and Marine

1. **You're in a committed relationship, but oops, you've consummated a fatal attraction. Your next step is:**
   a) Announce the relationship is over. Plan a commitment ceremony with your new love.
   b) Say nothing to your lover, and be sure to ignore the person when you run into them.
   c) Say nothing, but try to interest your significant other in a three-way.
   d) Confess all and have a heavy discussion of monogamy, all the while secretly planning your next tryst.
   e) Brag that you shagged Sharon Stone.

2. **You've been dating for a while. Now it's time to make the big move, so you:**
   a) Check local domestic partnership laws.
   b) Invite them to join your summer share.
   c) Give them a detailed description of everyone you've ever slept with.
   d) Confess your secret desire for Maribou mules to vacuum in.
   e) Invite them back to your place to admire your beer can pyramid.

3. **You've brought someone home and now realize that they don't look nearly as sexy as they did back at the:**
   a) Menstrual extraction workshop.
   b) Dungeon.
   c) Lollapalooza.
   d) Barneys Warehouse Sale.
   e) Sports bar.

4. **You're in the video store and—confess!—you've got a jones on for some porno. You select:**
   a) *Thelma and Louise* (for the parking lot scene).
   b) *Falcon Videopac No. 71.*
   c) *Querelle.*
   d) *Erotic in Nature.*
   e) *America's Dirtiest Home Videos, No. 32.*

5.   Madonna is:
a)   A tool of the patriarchy.
b)   A life-style choice.
c)   God.
d)   An empowered appropriator of dominant postmodern signifiers.
e)   A scary lesbo.

6.   Plates should be:
a)   Eaten off of.
b)   Tastefully decorated with a British Empire pink tea rose pattern.
c)   Collected from souvenir shops on road trips.
d)   Festooned with a neo-Constructivist pattern.
e)   In your lighted curio cabinet.

7.   It's all about shoes, and shoes are all about:
a)   Comfort.
b)   A high, spiked heel.
c)   An open toe.
d)   A tough, streetwise look.
e)   Anything in bone, or white.

8.   You've won a $10,000 shopping spree, so:
a)   You go haywire on the phone to Patagonia and donate the remainder to wymynspace.
b)   Your personal shopper at Bergdorf's can expect a call.
c)   The range at Banana Republic is endless.
d)   Donna Karan is about to get even richer.
e)   Jaclyn Smith will never have to do another shampoo commercial as long as she lives.

9.   Leather is
a)   Murder.
b)   A life-style.
c)   Totally hot.
d)   A perfect statement on crisp fall nights.
e)   What you wish your La-Z-Boy was covered in.

10.   You sleep on:
a)   A futon from Arise.
b)   A high-tech sleeping platform upholstered in black leather.
c)   Ikea's genius tubular chrome number.
d)   The 18th-century sleigh-bed you rescued from that barn sale.
e)   A knotty pine colonial from Ethan Allen.

11. **When you think flowers, you think:**
a) Georgia O'Keeffe.
b) Pastel gladiolas in an Art Deco repro vase.
c) A single live white orchid.
d) Pink anthuriums.
e) Merlin Olsen.

12. **A vacation is a good time to:**
a) Strap the bikes to the roof of the Tercel and haul ass to Michigan.
b) Fall into a K-hole.
c) Enjoy a weeklong Russ Meyer video fest.
d) Sample the cuisine, mudbaths, and heartbreaking vistas of Napa and Sonoma.
e) Visit Six Flags, Disney World—the sky's the limit!

13. **You drive:**
a) A late model Honda Prelude.
b) A '69 lemon Eldorado with white interior.
c) A black Jeep.
d) A black Saab turbo with black interior.
e) A Ford Taurus.

14. **Your favorite movie is:**
a) *Desert Hearts*.
b) *Falcon Videopac No. 5*.
c) *Truth or Dare*.
d) *A Walk on the Wild Side*.
e) Anything with Kevin Costner.

15. **You read (besides *Out*):**
a) The CISPES newsletter.
b) *World of Interiors*.
c) The J. Crew catalog.
d) *Mirabella*.
e) *Parade*.

16. **A meal is:**
a) Cooked in one pot and lasts the week.
b) Low fat, high carb—sushi is an excellent choice.
c) Mission burritos, and don't skimp on the margaritas!
d) Grilled fish and chilled chardonnay.
e) The San Francisco treat.

17.   San Francisco is:
a)   It's not San Francisco, it's the Bay Area.
b)   The place you moved after sleeping with everyone in New York and L.A.
c)   A great place for a communal Ecstasy rave.
d)   The place your lover moved after they slept with everyone in New York and L.A.
e)   Lobster bibs on Fisherman's Wharf.

18.   Free-association: When you think of Camille, you think:
a)   How underappreciated Andrea Dworkin and Catherine MacKinnon are.
b)   How divine Greta Garbo looked surrounded by all that Pratesi linen.
c)   Sisterhood is powerful, especially if you're a supermodel.
d)   Of her movie with Lauren Hutton.
e)   Of a very destructive hurricane back in '69.

19.   You work at:
a)   A battered-women's shelter.
b)   Oribe.
c)   Your own psychotherapy practice.
d)   A tastefully appointed design and home-furnishings atelier.
e)   Cracker Barrel.

20.   The holiday season is a time to:
a)   Celebrate Kwanza with a multicultural mosaic of friends.
b)   Slide into a K-hole.
c)   Have dinner at the Century in South Beach.
d)   Be drawn into a pointless fight with your father about the ERA.
e)   Argue over whose family to stay with.

Scoring: For every a) answer, give yourself 10 points. For every b), 6 points. For every c), 4 points. For every d), 2. For every e), 0.

160-200 Points: TO-THE-LETTER DYKE. Oh, sister, you are *wommon*, we hear you roar. Keep fighting the good fight, but we wonder, don't you ever want to steal away from the collective for a day of pampering at the local Kut 'n' Kurl? We won't tell. Promise.

120-158 Points: BY-THE-BOOK FAG. "Daddy-O-Daddy why you treat 'em so mean, you're the hottest Daddy that they've ever seen." We love you hard-partying butches, but even Tom of Finland's boys doffed those uniforms once in a while. So why not slip out of your harness?

80-118 Points: DYKEY-FAG. You're a little bit lesbo, you're a little bit rock 'n' roll, you happenin' PC hipster you. You like the good life, with a rough edge. But even tired old clones need love too. Load up the Bronco with your buds (girls too) and check out the local ACT UP meeting. You might run into the stereotypical gay male of your dreams.

40-78 Points: FAGGY-DYKE. You're a thoroughly postmodern Millie. Lipstick doesn't scare you—and neither does that easy-come-and-go approach to the nasty that your bros. have raised to a high art. Just remember, sooner or later the bills come due—on your heart and, of course, your credit card.

0-38 Points: GET A CLUE. The magazine you're looking for is *Outside*, not *Out*.

THE BACHELOR

HAVE A PARTY

While writer and editor Andrew Sullivan can be flip about the travails of his bachelorhood, he is quite serious in his appraisal of same-sex marriage. "The core of our exclusion is the exclusion from the most important institution which cele-brates and affirms love," he says. Following the legalization of same-sex marriage "and a couple of other things," he says, "I think we should have a party and close down the gay rights movement for good."

Deb Schwartz

PHOTO: Jack Pierson

COAST TO COAST

WHERE WE GO	WHERE THEY GO
Key West	Key Largo
South Beach	South Jersey
Fire Island	Coney Island
Provincetown	Providence
Disneyland	Historic Williamsburg
Michigan Womyn's Music Festival	Michigan's Mackinaw Island
Vassar	Texas A&M
Aspen	Boulder
Santa Fe	Scottsdale
West Hollywood	Planet Hollywood
Palm Springs	Palm Beach
Russian River	Russia
Hell	Purgatory

NEWSSTAND

WHAT WE READ

Allure
Mademoiselle
Details
The New York Times
Men's Fitness
US
Vanity Fair
The New Yorker
Buzz
Steam

GAY LIFE

WHAT WE STOLE FROM THEM

WHAT THEY STOLE FROM US

WHAT WE STOLE FROM THEM	WHAT THEY STOLE FROM US
Abba	RuPaul
Rock Hudson	Liberace
Hair bleaching	Body piercing
Head shaving	Caesar haircuts
Tattoos	Goatees and sideburns
Work boots (1970s)	Work boots (1990s)
Tommy Lee Jones	Jaye Davidson
Punk	Disco
Barbra Streisand	Melissa Etheridge
Batman	*Interview with the Vampire*
Keg parties	Quiche
A Course in Miracles	Feminist movement
Halloween (from their kids)	Halloween (from our ghettos)

WHAT THEY READ

Vogue
Glamour
GQ
The Washington Times
Sports Illustrated
People
Esquire
New York magazine
Los Angeles magazine
Screw

STRAIGHT LIFE

WHERE HAVE WE BEEN

1968 • Mart Crowley's *The Boys in the Band* opens in New York

1969 • Police prepare for a routine raid of New York's Stonewall Inn, which turns into a riot in the wee hours of the next morning. This fierce reaction to the bar raid marks the beginning of the modern lesbian and gay civil rights movement

1970 • First Gay Pride march, New York City

1972 • First openly gay delegates, Jim Foster and Madeline Davis, speak at the Democratic National Convention

1973 • First person to come out on national television: Lance Loud on *An American Family*, PBS
• The American Psychiatric Association removes homosexuality from classification as an illness

1974 • Introduction of first federal gay rights bill (as yet unpassed) in U.S. House of Representatives
• First lesbian writers conference, Chicago

1976 • First gay character in major U.S. comic strip: Andy Lippincott in Garry Trudeau's *Doonesbury*
• *A Chorus Line*—the Broadway musical featuring the stories of gay male entertainers—wins the Pulitzer Prize for drama
• "Tales of the City" by Armistead Maupin first appears in *The San Francisco Chronicle*, complete with homosexual characters mixing happily with the West Coast mainstream

1977 • Members of the three-year-old National Gay Task Force meet with an aide to President Jimmy Carter
• Anita Bryant leads denunciations as Miami passes first gay right ordinance in a southern U.S. city

1978 • First "Gay Night" at Disneyland

1979   • Dan White found innocent of murder in assassination of Mayor George
          Moscone and fellow San Francisco Supervisor Harvey Milk, the city's
          first elected gay leader; protest turns into a riot
        • Teenager Aaron Fricke takes a male date to his senior prom after win-
          ning that right in court, Rhode Island
        • The Village People's subtly gay-themed final hit single "In the Navy"
          begins a 13-week run in *Billboard*'s Top 40
        • 100,000 attend the national lesbian and gay rights march on Washington

1981   • *The New York Times* reports an outbreak of Kaposi's sarcoma, a rare
          skin cancer, in gay men

1982   • Larry Kramer, Edmund White, and four others found Gay Men's
          Health Crisis, New York, to address the reports of "Gay-Related
          Immune Deficiency" (GRID)
        • First Gay Games, San Francisco
        • Cris Williamson and Meg Christian become the first openly gay
          or lesbian act to play Carnegie Hall

1984   • Boy George accepts Culture Club's Grammy for Best New Artist by
          telling Americans, "You know a good drag queen when you see one"

1985   • First classes held at New York's city-funded Harvey Milk School for
          gay, lesbian, and bisexual youth
        • Rock Hudson dies, stirring mainstream interest in AIDS for the first time

1986   • In *Bowers vs. Hardwick*, by a 5-4 decision, the U.S. Supreme Court
          refuses to declare anti-sodomy laws unconstitutional

1987   • First major demonstration of the AIDS Coalition to Unleash Power
          (ACT UP), New York
        • 650,000 attend the national March on Washington
        • Death of Bayard Rustin, gay and civil rights activist

1988   • Second Gay Games, Vancouver

1989
- First gay U.S. Postal Service cancellation, "Stonewall Sta.," New York
- First state-sanctioned gay marriages, Denmark

1990
- *OutWeek* magazine outs the late multimillionaire Malcolm Forbes
- *Common Threads: Stories from the Quilt* wins Academy Award for Best Documentary, bringing greater national attention to the "AIDS Quilt"
- First U.S. bill to mention "sexual orientation," the Hate Crime Statistics Act, signed into law by President George Bush.
- Five hundred attend the first major demonstration of the direct action activist group Queer Nation, New York

1991
- *L.A. Law*'s "lesbian kiss," between C.J. and Abby, airs on network television and stirs delight and outrage
- San Francisco becomes the first city to register same-sex couples as domestic partners
- Marlon Riggs' *Tongues Untied*, featuring African-American gay men, airs on many PBS stations

1992
- *Out* magazine opens its offices, New York
- Candidate Bill Clinton tells gay and lesbian supporters, "I have a vision of America and you are part of it"

1993
- At a Clinton inaugural ball Melissa Etheridge announces she is a lesbian
- One million attend the national March on Washington
- President Bill Clinton reverses himself and allows the military to enforce a "Don't ask, don't tell" policy against lesbian and gay service members
- Tony Kushner's *Angels in America: Millennium Approaches* opens on Broadway and becomes the first AIDS-themed drama to win the Pulitzer Prize

1996
- Judge Kevin Chang rules that Hawaii has no "compelling state interest" in preventing same-sex marriages, opening the way for lesbian and gay unions to be legalized
- Congress passes and President Clinton signs the Defense of Marriage Act that allows states not to recognize same-sex marriage

PASSIONATE COMMITMENT

Somehow you'd expect a pair of public interest lawyers to be deadly serious, but get them off policy questions and Paula Ettelbrick (right), legislative counsel at Empire State Pride Agenda, New York's gay rights lobby, and Suzanne Goldberg, a staff attorney at Lambda Legal Defense and Education Fund, cannot stop laughing together. Goldberg deadpans, "We met in the summer of 1989. In a bar." The two crack up, and Ettelbrick says, "Suzanne! That's not quite the whole story." After several years of friendship the two got together, and along with a passionate commitment to fighting for the rights of lesbians and gay men and a love of New York City, they now share a small apartment in Greenwich Village.

PHOTO: Aldo Rossi

While both women advocate the right to marry as a matter of policy, they don't view it as the be-all and end-all of gay activism, nor as a choice they would make personally. "I wouldn't want the state to be involved in sanctioning or regulating my relationship," Goldberg says. "I want the glue holding my relationship together to be my love and my personal sense of commitment." The two share "a terrific synergy" professionally and look forward to growing old together. "Sometimes we joke about getting old and having Girl Scouts help us cross the street," says Ettelbrick.

Deb Schwartz

BEF
THE
REVOI

ORE

Kay Tobin Lahusen (left) and Barbara Gittings

José Sarria

UTION

PEOPLE ON THE GAY AND LESBIAN FRONTIER

If gay pioneers have one feature in common, it is this: They were there—before most of us knew there was a there or, knowing, rushed off in the opposite direction. To stand up insistently for who one was during the pre-Stonewall years required—given the overwhelmingly negative view of homosexuality—most uncommon self-regard (with a strong admixture of scorn for authority).

Where did the confidence to take these courageous stands come from? We can never fully know. Why some people, against all odds, do not succumb to standard socialization is among the many mysteries of human personality. Thus the small segment of children from poverty-stricken abusive homes who do not go under but actually thrive. Thus those sexual and gender non-conformists in rural areas or small towns with no background or training in public speech or political work, who will suddenly, dazzlingly, stand up to oppression—despite the lack of support networks or media attention, and in the face of very real violence.

How lucky for the rest of us that they did—and do—exist.

Martin Duberman

Harry Hay

"I had this idea that all the other sissies should come together and find out who we were," says Hay about founding the Mattachine Society, one of the first gay organizations, in Los Angeles in 1950. Hay's account of Mattachine's early days, along with his other writings, are collected in *Radically Gay*, published by Beacon Press.

Jim Kepner

"When I first heard the word *homosexual* horribly defined, I realized this was a political question for us to deal with," recalls Kepner. "We had to do something about changing the horrible situation homosexuals were in." A writer for *ONE* magazine, an early gay publication, during the 1950s, Kepner founded and remains a board member of *ONE* Institute/ International Gay and Lesbian Archives, a huge repository of gay and lesbian historical material.

Sylvia Rivera

As a founder of the Street Transvestite Action Revolutionaries in 1971, Rivera gave young transgendered hustlers the support she had lacked. When the Stonewall riots erupted, she was there, hurling change and insults at the cops with the best of them. Rivera, recalls, "What gave me the power at the time was that I was involved in the peace movement, the civil rights movement, and the women's movement, and when it did happen, the night of the Stonewall riot, it was time for gay people to stand up for our rights."

Luvenia Pinson

Pinson was a veteran of the Harlem "rent party" circuit, where black lesbians had long met and socialized, when she helped found Salsa Soul Sisters in 1974. Through parties, dances, and demonstrations, the group launched a network of lesbians of color that continues today under the banner of African Ancestral Lesbians United for Societal Change. "A lot of talent came out of that group," says Pinson.

Dr. Evelyn Hooker

In l945 Hooker's unprecedented study of gay men provided the first scientific evidence challenging the widely held belief linking homosexuality and psychopathology. "If the established order says I'm wrong, and I know I'm right, nothing can budge me from my position," says Hooker. "Working with and in the gay community has been an extraordinary experience."

Rev. Robert W. Wood

"I was told, 'You'll never get it published,'" says Wood of his groundbreaking 1960 book, *Christ and the Homosexual*, the first sympathetic study of gay men and lesbians in the church. An openly gay ordained pastor in the United Church of Christ for 35 years and now retired, Wood says, "I'd grown up in a Christian home, and began to look to the church for guidance. There was nothing [on homosexuality] in the books in the seminary library. I realized I was going to have to write the book myself."

Phyllis Lyon and Del Martin

Longtime partners Lyon and Martin were among the founders of Daughters of Bilitis, conceived in l955 as a secret club to widen members' social circles. Over time DOB evolved into the first lesbian political organization. "Before we could have a movement we had to convince our members they weren't illegal, immoral, and sick, which was what we were told at the time," says Lyon. "During those early years we did a lot of peer counseling," says Martin.

José Sarria

"I must have been out of my mind. I could have been arrested or harassed, but I had the courage of 25 queens," says Sarria, the first openly gay man to run for public office (in 1961) and founder of The Imperial Court, an organization of fund-raising female and male impersonators. A longtime entertainer, Sarria, currently emcees *The Widow Norton's Bar Tour*, a San Francisco pub crawl and cabaret act.

Barbara Gittings and Kay Tobin Lahusen

"I loved belonging to a special people, but I wanted to do away with the closet," says Gittings. The pair met in 1961 at a Daughters of Bilitis picnic. Gittings founded the New York chapter of DOB, and Lahusen documented much of the movement's early history in reporting and photography.

Stormé DeLarverié

"Somebody said it couldn't be done and I disagreed. *Can't* isn't in my dictionary." As singer, emcee, and manager for the cabaret Jewel Box Revue during the 1950s and '60s, DeLarverié cut a strikingly handsome figure in her formal male attire. "[The revue members] asked me to join them, and I said, 'I'll come over for six months,' and I stayed for 14 years." DeLarverié regularly works security at lesbian clubs in New York City.

Jeanne Manford

When Manford marched with her gay activist son, Morty, in the second annual Christopher Street Liberation Day parade in 1972, she broke new ground, and her support for her son led to the eventual formation of PFLAG—Parents, Friends, and Families of Lesbians and Gays. "I just loved my son and knew there could be nothing wrong [with him]," she says simply. An elementary school teacher for many years, Manford is now retired. Morty died of AIDS in 1992, at age 42.

Frank Kameny

Fired from his job at the U.S. Army Map Service in 1957 because he is gay, this Harvard-educated astronomist took his case against the Civil Service Commission all the way up to the Supreme Court, which declined to hear it. (The policy was finally, quietly, changed in 1975.) Founder of the independent Washington [D.C.] Mattachine Society, Kameny remains a fighter. "I have chosen not to adjust myself to society but, with considerable success, to adjust society to me."

Lisa Ben

Beginning in 1947, Lisa Ben—her pseudonym an anagram of lesbian— produced nine editions of *Vice Versa*, a "magazine for gay gals." In her spare time as a secretary during the era before photocopying, Ben laboriously produced 10 copies by stuffing her typewriter with 4 carbon copies and typing the entire magazine through twice. She distributed it by hand. Ben recalls, "After I got rolling with it, I got asked out and met a lot of girls and had a great time."

LISA BEN

WHAT
R
DO
WE
WANT

GHTS

?

What Do Gay Men & Lesbians Want?

Lack of access to marriage and its rights; state ballots that deem us "abnormal and perverse;" discriminatory workplace policies such as those practiced by the military; AIDS, breast cancer, and the disastrous lack of national health care; hate crimes; the ubiquity of bell-bottoms—the list of our battles goes on, and our need to construct strong, unified alliances to fight them is almost as daunting as the threats they pose to our basic rights. Since before the 1993 March on Washington, we have learned we will win only when in numbers. But what can we agree on? Can we even, say, agree to disagree? Some of our best, brightest, and most irreverent gave their answers on the eve of the historic march.

Linda Villarosa, editor, *Essence* magazine: All the privileges straight people enjoy, only we'll exercise them with more class, style, and compassion.

Joan Nestle, Lesbian Herstory Archives: Recently we've been saying "we're just like you," but what I consider history-making is "No, we are not just like you." Our difference is our contribution to the human family.

Quentin Crisp, author, *The Naked Civil Servant*: All the straight people I know say, "What do the queers want now?" because they feel they've done so much for them, and of course they have. I don't expect anything. People are always saying they've got rights. They don't have rights. If we all got what we deserved, we'd all starve. Everyone should say, "I am nothing. I deserve nothing." Then everything after that would be a bonus.

Donna Redwing, Portland, Oregon, activist: Basic human civil rights. But if things don't move more quickly, we should ask for reparations. That always sends a chill up the spine of most straights.

The Lady Bunny: Sense enough to lose interest in the military. Whatever happened to flower arranging and hairdressing?

Barney Frank, U.S. Representative, Massachusetts: Gays want what every other citizen wants, to pursue his or her business without oppression or being harassed. When they march in the streets they should send three letters: one to their Representative, one to each Senator, maybe even to be delivered by hand.

Michelangelo Signorile, author, *Queer In America*: Total control.

Marvin Leibman, former editor, *The National Review*: For an old guy like me, I need a boyfriend. Gay men and lesbians need to trust no politician, including Bill Clinton, but to infiltrate into all aspects of political life.

Barbara Smith, publisher, Kitchen Table:Women of Color Press: The question is different if you're a well-off white gay man as opposed to a working class lesbian of color; the issues are entirely different. As a lesbian of color, what I need is a revolution.

Kate Clinton, lesbian humorist: ① Tupperware with matching tops. ② Perfectly positioned side mirrors. ③ Full human rights.

Ann Northrop, activist: ① All the land west of the Mississippi. ② A month in the sun. ③ A little screwdriver to pry our minds open, so we can acknowledge that we really are a diverse community and can begin to appreciate that and respect each other. ④ Self-respect. ⑤ A sense of entitlement. ⑥ Our own TV channels so we can have the same communication tools as the Religious Right. ⑦ Decent wardrobes. ⑧ A roof over everybody's head, food to eat, jobs, cures for breast cancer and AIDS. ⑨ A lesbian President of the United States.

Sarah Schulman, author, *Rat Bohemia*: Universal mind expansion, retribution, and peace.

Cheryl Clarke, poet: Institutionalize lesbian-feminist leadership.

Dorothy Allison, author, *Bastard Out of Carolina*: The list of my wants is exceeded only by the list of things I don't have.

Donna Minkowitz, journalist: An end to gender as we know it, and a complete transformation of all social institutions to make room for the pursuit of pleasure.

PHOTO: Joshua Jordan

Mark Welsh, screenwriter (left), and John Bartlett, fashion designer

John Bartlett, fashion designer: Personally speaking, what we all really want is a live-in macrobiotic chef trained in the art of shiatsu and hair-tinting.

Jacqueline Woodson, writer: Tattoos we don't hate in ten years like the Elton John-inspired butterfly on my back and the unicorn on my friend Louise's butt.

Paul Rudnick, playwright: Gay people want: ① To be able to legally adopt their leather jackets.

(2) Federal reparations for having had to take gym in junior high (except for lesbians, for whom field hockey was the equivalent of a back room activity). (3) Exemption from military service, due to giggling. (4) More spreads in *Metropolitan Home* on interior designer couples who "can't abide clutter" and have opted for just "one or two perfect things." (5) A public forum on "Does HIV cause independent movie deals?"

Isaac Mizrahi, fashion designer: Aside from a cure for AIDS? Gays and lesbians want archetypes, fabulous shining examples. They want to be able to go to the movies and figure out how to lead their lives.

Simon Levay, researcher: For the gene that determines sexual orientation to be discovered.

Debra Chasnoff, Oscar-winning filmmaker, *Deadly Deception*: I would like to see mandatory homophobia prevention education integrated into elementary and secondary school curricula.

Nina Jacobson, Vice-President, Production, Universal Pictures: To have a new word for lesbian, preferably something that doesn't rhyme with thespian.

Tony Kushner, playwright, *Angels in America*: I am into being specific these days so I called some friends and asked them what they wanted. Stephen wants Jeff Stryker and beauty, beauty, beauty. Eduardo wants more than being legal in the army and for gays to stop being so middle class. Rosemary wants her son not to be discriminated against for having gay parents. Bob wants a house with a yard. Alva wants a unified field of queer theory. Janice wants Alva. Lea wants a job. I want my civil rights and my boyfriend to move to New York.

Allen Ginsberg, poet: Sexuality's loose not fixed. Legalize it.

Stuart Elliot, advertising columnist, *The New York Times*: Equality—and to be left alone.

Jewelle Gomez, author, *The Gilda Stories*: Lesbian feminists want the destruction of Western civilization as we know it, reexamination of the issues of power in our society, and a redesign of the institutions and offices that exert power in our society.

John Rechy, author, *City of Night*: I look forward to the time when everyone, including ourselves, stops asking, What creates homosexuals? That question is relevant only if the question, What creates heterosexuals? is given equal attention. The first question assumes that we deviate from what is "acceptable"—a deadly sophistry that establishes only heterosexuality as acceptable. I will not mind being identified as a "self-avowed gay writer" when John Updike is routinely identified as "a self-avowed heterosexual writer."

PHOTO: Lego

As one of the three couples whose case, *Baehr vs. Lewin*, challenges the constitutionality of same-sex marriage in Hawaii, Genora Dancel (left) and Ninia Baehr have called into question the institution of marriage as a hetero-only proposition. Neither woman planned it that way. Baehr's mother introduced them, a moment Baehr recalls as love at first sight. Three months later the two women called the gay community center in Honolulu in search of information: Could they designate each other as beneficiaries on their life insurance policies? What about sharing health insurance coverage? The man on the other end of the line was activist Bill Woods, who launched the court case and encouraged the couple to participate. "We've accepted the responsibility of marriage: in sickness and in health and all that kind of stuff, but we want the safeguards," says Baehr.   **Deb Schwartz**

CANDACE GINGRICH

He was born in 1943. She was born in 1966. To help Candace remember how she was related to this man who only visited on holidays, their mother referred to him as "Brother Newt." But the brother who became Speaker of the House was present year-round in the family scrapbook dedicated to his political successes. Pulling out from under his shadow wasn't easy.

Candace's political epiphany came at a family Thanksgiving dinner in 1994. A sister asked how she felt about their brother's published comment that "it would be madness to pretend that families are anything other than heterosexual couples." Unable to reply, Candace began to research Newt's actual politics. Dismayed, she transformed herself into Candace the Menace, the dyke-next-door with that cheery smile, reminding America that even Kulturkampf Republicans' families value their own happy homos.

E. J. Graff

SISTER ACT

Jamie Nabozny is barely old enough to drink in many states, but he already knows more about the legal system than most adults. After five years of beatings and verbal harassment for being gay in Ashland, Wisconsin, junior high and high schools, he's had his day in court, winning nearly a million-dollar judgment.

PHOTO: Ann Marsden

According to court documents, Nabozny was "hit, kicked, and spat upon in school hallways, bathrooms, locker rooms, and other facilities," and subjected to frequent verbal harassment. In one particularly bad episode, two students pushed him to the floor, "taunted him, and acted out a mock rape on him." Nabozny claims that the principal told him, "Boys will be boys," and told his parents that if he "was going to be openly gay that [he] had to expect that kind of stuff." (The principal has denied making the comments.)

The appellate decision is "earth-shaking," according to David Buckel, of Lambda Legal Defense and Education Fund, one of Nabozny's lawyers. "It essentially sends the message to school principals that they can no longer tolerate anti-gay abuse in schools."

"Politics has become a very big part of my life. It's not something that's a passion for me," says Nabozny with a shrug. Eventually, he wants to work with gay teens to help them experience the kind of adolescence that he missed out on, and he hopes "to get married and have kids"—perhaps by the time he reaches the ripe old age of 30.   **Bruce Shenitz**

GAYS IN THE MILITARY

The 1993 controversy over the right of lesbians and gay men to remain in the military brought us the "Don't ask, don't tell" policy—under which more people have been expelled than under the old regulations. "I can't believe we risk our lives, we take an oath to protect the Constitution, and the only right we have is the right to keep your mouth shut," said "Susan," who would not speak with her full name when she sought to leave the military. "It's like this moral blackmail—as long as you lie, OK, but if you try to stand up for yourself and who you are, then your ass is grass, you go back to the sorry little town you came from. I made a top-10 list of things I won't miss about the military, and number one is, now I can kiss girls without going to jail."

"My conscience was just putting me in a real bind," said Air Force Captain Richard Richenberg. "I realized the possible risk I was taking by coming out, but I weighed that against my personal integrity and what we were taught as officers—that you're supposed to help people get over prejudice."

Hundreds of wrecked lives later, it's clear that the new policy either maintains the status quo, or, in many cases, pushes gay men and lesbians back. One service member was recently challenged. "Are you a fucking faggot?" "Yes, sir," he responded. "Sir, you're not supposed to ask, but since you did, yes, sir, I am." "Asking" clearly continues, even in the age of "Don't ask, don't tell."

Sara Miles

CIVIL DEFENSE

Emergency Services for Service Members

"Don't ask, don't tell" won't protect you. If you're under investigation, facing discharge, being threatened, or thinking of coming out, please remember:

KNOW YOUR LEGAL RIGHTS

Article 31 of the Uniform Code of Military Justice gives you the right to remain silent.

SAY NOTHING

All statements, even those to doctors and chaplains, or private conversations with friends, can be used against you.

SIGN NOTHING

Even your initials can waive your legal rights.

GET LEGAL HELP

The new regulations are tricky—don't go it alone. Organizations that provide confidential help include: Service Members Legal Defense Network, 202-328-3244, and the Military Law Task Force, 619-233-1701.

NONDISCRIMINATION MADE EASY

More and more gay men and lesbians can go to their jobs secure in the knowledge that they cannot be fired for keeping a lover's photo on their desks or dancing with a same-sex partner at the company Christmas party. Others are not so lucky—yet.

Corporations may seem like behemoths impervious to change, but as a shareholder you can have potent powers of persuasion. "To qualify for filing a shareholder resolution for something like a nondiscrimination policy," says Franklin Research and Development's Shelley Alpern, "you only have to own $1,000 worth of that stock for at least a year before filing." Patrick Doherty, director of investment responsibility for New York City Comptroller, observes, "If you're a member of a labor union, a student or graduate of a college or university, or a citizen of a state or city, you have a right to ask how [that institution] votes on its stock." Alpern adds that "just proposing a resolution and giving it a lot of publicity can be enough to get a company to negotiate."

• Start the process by writing to the CEO at least a year ahead of the next annual meeting to ask if the company has a written nondiscrimination policy. If not, when does it plan to implement one?
• Cite the good business reasons for doing so: the company is cutting itself off from an excellent pool of employees; it could be offending a big chunk of its consumer base.
• Be persistent, follow up, emphasize how many shares you control, and hint that you're considering a shareholder resolution—which millions of others will see and start to ask about.
• Get help in correctly structuring the process and paperwork so company lawyers won't nitpick and demolish the resolution immediately. The Wall Street Project, a gay workplace activist group [P.O. Box 387, New York, NY 10028; (212) 289-1741], can provide assistance free of charge.

Ed Mickens

THE NEXT CIVIL RIGHTS FRONTIER

Nobody knows how many gay men and lesbians became parents before coming out—estimates range from 2 million to 8 million. The numbers have climbed as more parents have come out. But most never enter the heralded halls of justice at all. The lucky ones are able to strike an amicable arrangement with their ex-spouses without a trial. More often, parents avoid court precisely because they fear their sexuality being exposed and used against them.

The Lavender Families Network grew out of efforts begun by lesbians in the 1970s who set up defense funds to help women battling custody cases. "It's a good model that can be expanded," suggests legal activist Paula Ettelbrick. Lesbians and gay men can become more aggressive about cases where there's a blatant discrimination: attending courtroom hearings, holding public demonstrations, getting involved in judicial education, setting up judicial screening panels to rate judges running for election, and holding accountable the politicians who pick judges.

Alisa Solomon

GAY PARENTING

On a perfect June day in Washington in 1995, more than 50 lesbian and gay elected officials arrived at the gate to 1600 Pennsylvania Avenue. Invited to the White

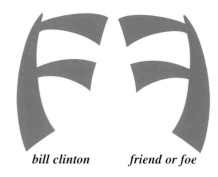

bill clinton *friend or foe*

House for a meeting with Cabinet-level power players from the Clinton administration, they were looking forward to a historic event. Instead, they were greeted by Secret Service employees wearing blue rubber gloves.

Ushered inside, the gay officials seethed. As White House staffers stuttered out apologies and tried to convince the group of Clinton's goodwill, the unmistakable voice of an extremely irritated queen rang out. "Don't expect us to genuflect," snapped Tom Ammiano, a city supervisor from San Francisco. "OK?" He stood up, his voice rising. "Basically, you're saying this is what we've done for you, and don't forget it. OK, we all want to support the president. But you walk a mile in our pumps before you tell us how grateful we should be." Even as he was re-elected, Bill Clinton had at best an uneasy relationship with American lesbians and gay men. Few people could wholeheartedly accept his 1992 claim: "What I came here today to tell you in simple terms is I have a vision, and you are a part of it." **Sara Miles**

ILLUSTRATION: Jarret Huddleston

CYBER ACTIVISM

The Internet can be an activist's best pal. Think of cyberspace as a virtual post office; once you know someone's E-mail address, you can correspond with them, forward mail, create global chain letters and petition drives and use your own Web site to let the world know what you want done on lesbian and gay rights. Here's a start on getting the message out.

What's the buzz?

Getting clear and accurate information is an important step on the road to activism. You can send an E-mail message with your E-mail address in it to your favorite wired group and ask them to hook you up (although the staff might hate you for this). True sophisticates can send a "subscribe" message to the list's E-mail address, and the person or computer in charge of the list will sign you up. The Queer Resources Directory on the Web (http://www.qrd.org/QRD/), which catalogs just about every same-sex, on-line option under the sun, is a great place to discover E-mail mailing lists.

Posting to boards, talking in chat rooms

Commercial Internet providers, like America Online, have tons
of their own internal electronic message boards, organized by
category; any subscriber can read and post messages on them.
On the larger Internet, newsgroups (discussion groups on a particular topic) work on a similar principle. In order to post your
own message there, you have to subscribe to that newsgroup in
the same way you did when you signed up for Action Alert. If
you're posting a call to action, remember: Include a cutoff date,
otherwise your missive might float around the Internet until the
end of time.

How to get a politician's attention

Petitions are OK, form letters are better, individualized letters
are the best. (Remember: If you're sending around a sample letter or petition, include instructions on how, for instance, a person might affix his or her name to the document and where to
send a signed version.)

Finding addresses for elected officials

The White House has its own homepage (http://www.white-house.gov), as do most state and local governments. A good way to find these home pages is to enter the name of your state into the information slot on a Web browser and see what comes up.

How to design an action alert

To send out an E-mail action alert, make sure the phrasing is clear and punchy. "You need to use very specific information that tells people, 'This is what's happening' and 'This is what you need to do about it,'" says Heidi C. Scanlon, electronic media coordinator of the Washington, D.C.-based AIDS Action Council (http://www.thebody.com).

Evaluation

Want to know if your cyber campaign actually worked? Ask people to cc (carbon copy) you the E-mail letters they send.

Liz Galst

WEB SITES WITH BITE

WebActive: http://www.webactive.com
A weekly updated guide to what's new in activism on-line.

Youth Action OnLine: http://www.youth.org
The personal and the political: how to find a pen pal, deal with coming out, action alerts for a host of subjects.

National Gay and Lesbian Task Force: http://www.ngltf.org
White papers and reports on topics ranging from hate crime to gay marriage.

Transexual Menace International:
http://www.echonyc.com/~degrey/Menace.html
Upcoming events, chapters throughout North America, T-shirts with their gory logo.

ACT UP/New York: http://www.actupny.org
The usual great graphics, plus a primer on hounding state officials and executives in the pharmaceutical industry around AIDS treatment issues.

Women's Health:
http://sunsite.unc.edu/cheryb/women/resource/healthint.html
Every women's health issue under the sun.

National Black Gay and Lesbian Leadership Forum:
http://qrd.rdrop.com:80/qrd/www/orgs/nbgllf/
Activities of the country's only national black gay and lesbian organization.

HOW DO

WE LIVE

In June 1969, when a contingent of gay men left the hidden interior
of the Stonewall Inn, emerged into the bright street light of
Greenwich Village, and smashed the beer bottle that would be heard
around the world, they illustrated perfectly how gay lib will always,
on some level, repeat a movement from now-you-don't-see-it to now-
you-do.

When it comes to our social lives, lesbians and gay men have compen-
sated for our obscurity by inventing a whole pantheon of "signifiers"
—to cite the high-tech jargon used by French literary types to
describe any words or symbols that carry meaning—that proclaim
our proclivities.

Undoubtedly the most popular gay sign is the pink triangle. Despite
protests that gays have all-too-blithely lifted the pink triangle from
its mournful context in the Holocaust, where Nazis used it to identify
male homosexual prisoners in concentration camps, post-mod
activists have transformed the pink triangle into a household symbol
of queer desire. AIDS activists pulled a similar stunt vis-à-vis the
yellow ribbon—a military memento used most recently to bring to
mind soldiers of U.S. fortune in the Gulf War—when they developed
the ubiquitous and infinitely more progressive red ribbon.

Some lesbians have continued to plunder World War II symbolism by stringing black triangle pendants next to their pink counterparts, even though there exists considerable debate over whether the Nazis used them to designate lesbian captives.

Runner-up on the Top 40 list of pop gay symbols has to be the rainbow flag, which first appeared in San Francisco at the 1978 Gay and Lesbian Freedom Day parade. The enormous rainbow flag unveiled at Stonewall 25, not to mention the staggering amount of money that organizers raised to raise it, ensures the corporate status of this symbol   and the myriad rainbow accessories, such as Freedom Rings, it spawned—for years to come. Jesse Jackson, of course, recognized the multicultural symbolism of the flag when he borrowed it for the Rainbow Coalition, and queer leather aficionados have Betsy-Rossed a rainbow flag with a black stripe to signify their particular ties to that bind.

In her book *Another Mother Tongue*, lesbian sign-monger Judy Grahn goes so far as to suggest that lesbian and gay leather love goes back to the sacred status of animal skins in homoerotic pre-Christian faerie cults. In any case, cowhide—as well as boots, wallets on a chain, and motorcycles themselves—naturally appeal to a subculture that has experienced itself on the edges of the mainstream.

Let's linger on the fringe a bit. The erotic sign system of bandannas is the Rubik's Cube of gay culture. In the early days of gay culture, S/M gay men and lesbians invented an ever-lengthening list connecting specific erotic leanings with certain colors and positions of one's hankie.

Even though you can read about them now in glossy life-style magazines, piercings too took hold on the extremities, gay and straight, of mainstream culture. In fact, if you take into account the popularity among queers of tattoos and body-sculpting (a.k.a., lifting dumbbells), you might say that the body-qua-art is now, as it was in pre-Stonewall "physique" magazines, somewhat of a gay thang.

Finally, a few words should be said about that time-honored gay institution of drag. Drag—especially the must-have of any Miss Anything's ensemble, the wig, which I'm convinced she stole from stripper dress code in the first place—is the *primum mobile* of gay signifiers. Moreover, the popularity of RuPaul notwithstanding, lesbians have always demonstrated drag expertise. No one but a good butch gal so carefully picks out her boxer shorts, and then lets them protrude ever so slightly from the tops of her trousers.

If these gay signs and sigs seem a little more postmodern than the carbon-datable lambda letter, the neo-Amazonian labrys, and the oh-so-womany double-female symbol, which always struck this young dyke as a bit classical and scientific anyway, then rejoice. Their proliferation is itself a sign of the fact that gay invisibility is fast becoming a minor modern inconvenience. **Heather Findlay**

Les Chic

When the love that dared not speak its name wouldn't shut up already

The giant papier-maché head wobbled, then crashed off the goddess'
sloping shoulders seconds before she was to lead the Dyke March out
of Dupont Circle, past the White House to the Washington Monument.
While the ad hoc committee on lesbian visibility scrambled to reattach
the head, the march stalled in a pleasant, murmuring holding pattern,
a sea of see-and-be-seen. Faster than you could say "penile reattach-
ment," the job was done and the goddess streamed past us. We all
stepped off the curb, jostling for a position in her wake. A low, gravel-
ly chant spread across the crowd: "We're dykes! Don't touch us! We'll
hurt you!" I pulled up short and the women behind me walked up my
calves. Was this lesbian chic or pique?

The months leading up to the 1993 March on Washington had been a
feeding frenzy off the très chic. The binge continued long after the
fairy dust had settled. Daytime talk shows outdid themselves with lesbian topics. Segment producers spun their Rolodexes and shouted,
"Get me that lesbian who reads." Or, "Get me that lesbian who wears
lipstick." Then, "Get me that upbeat lesbian." Maria Shriver did her
best. Lynn (I'm So) Sherr tilted her head, squinted, and tried to
understand Northampton lesbians on *20/20*. The only way a spokesles-
bian could distinguish herself from the pack was to have a boyfriend.

On the developmental timeline of lesbo sapiens, this chic era follows hard on the heels of the stealth lesbian period, a murky subterranean era in which we were present but undetectable. No popular women were out. We played the lesbian lineage game at potlucks: "A friend of a friend of a friend saw her at a bar in L.A." We watched Lily Tomlin specials together and said, "Look, she's wearing purple." We were the purple menace purged from the women's movement. In the gay movement we were told, "When we say 'gay,' we mean 'lesbian' too."

Let's face it. There's a fine line between chic and freak. Chic is nothing. Sharon Bottoms lost custody of her child in Virginia. Advertisers pulled out of a CBS *Schoolbreak Special* about prejudice against a teenager with two mommies. And Denver, in good old Colorado, home of antigay Amendment Two, refused to air it altogether. Recently I had to stare down a bubba at a doughnut-shop counter when he became annoyed at my extreme chicness and that of my companion.

That great feminist Mae West once snarled, "It is better to be looked over than overlooked." But all this lesbochic makes me nervous (color me ungrateful). It's too domesticating, too taming, too nice, too white. We're no longer dangerous; we're merely naughty. I say it's no time to be an Eddie Haskell lesbian. A lesbian is not a people pleaser. Chic is of the moment; radical is the momentum. When a woman chooses a woman, she may or may not be chic, but you can bet your ice pick she's radical.

Kate Clinton

Fire Island, New York—in the two adjacent communities Pines and Cherry Grove, Manhattan gay men and lesbian summer shareholders join with their compatriots from around the world to create the most intensely homo life available anywhere. Paradise for some; for others, a preamble to entering detox at the Pride Institute.

Key West, Florida—closer to Cuba than to Miami, the "Conch Republic" has long attracted gay and lesbian artists, writers, and other creative misfits. It boasts a well-established gay and lesbian community in what is one of the most beautiful small cities in America.

Ogonquit, Maine—the most laid-back lesbian and gay place on the continent, where a single dance club and a few good restaurants create an environment that is easeful and remote.

Palm Springs, California—home to U.S. Representative Sonny Bono, the Dinah Shore Golf Tournament, and many thong-optional gay male hostels, this desert oasis is the place Los Angeles goes when it wants to kick back and party hard.

Provincetown, Massachusetts—summer folk come here to be totally gay for a day or a week, sprawling on the beach, dancing at tea, gathering at Spiritus Pizza after the bars close—and hardier souls brave the isolation and cold to create one of America's year-round lesbian and gay small towns.

Russian River, California—otherwise known as the Guerneville metropolitan area, featuring a lovely but flood-prone river, this nook of redwoods nestled near the Pacific cliffs provides release from the stresses of America's gentlest big city, San Francisco.

South Beach, Florida—otherwise known as southern Miami Beach, or Chelsea in short pants, where there is more muscle and less fat per square inch of homosexual than anywhere else in America.

10 TIPS ON GETTING PICKED

1. Rather than emit the usual banal openers like "How ya doin'?" or "Want a date?", challenge your chosen target with things they couldn't hear from a prostitute. Pose esoteric queries about Stalin, multiculturalism, or the Middle East. You'll pique their curiosity, which is inexorably linked, in the long run, to their groin.

2. Wear something that could become a conversation piece, as long as it doesn't make the conversation become abusive. A little color, a little flounce, a little something other than the usual muscle-T might catch that special someone's roving eyeball. Draw the line at bad-taste-hall-of-fame stuff like acid-washed or ripped jeans.

3. Arrange to have a fake boyfriend or girlfriend hanging all over you. Everyone will suddenly want you because you're wanted by someone else and therefore must be worth having. Besides, a person who's already taken is so excitingly taboo.

4. Don't surround yourself with too many cute people, or too many people at all, except for that fake boy- or girlfriend. Don't wear shades (like I do). Don't wear lots of clothing or too much cologne (like I do). In fact, don't be like me at all. Instead, study old Lana Turner flicks and radiate willing sexuality. Be glamorous. Be loose. Be available. But . . .

5. Don't be *too* glamorous, loose, and available. Don't traipse across the dance floor on knee pads screaming "Free sex!" No one wants what they can all have.

6. Hold up a drink to that special someone's face and, with an endearing grimace, say, "Can you tell what this is?" Look like you really need to know the answer. If you don't get the person drunk, you'll at least get him or her engaged in some kind of twisted conversation that could lead to something even more twisted and personal.

7. Dance alone, casually bumping into people you like and slyly immersing yourself into their private spheres with a demented assurance. You'll be amazed at how easy it is to get them away from their partners.

8. For boys, feel their pecs admiringly and loudly gush, "Wow, you've really been working out!" In a room full of other self-absorbed muscle queens, they'll be glad someone noticed.

9. Totally dis the guy or gal of your choice in a major, obvious way, and pull the same outrageous stunt the next three nights you see them. On the fifth encounter, be mildly friendly, and they'll be yours.

10. Pounce.

Michael Musto

PHILL WILSON :

Phill Wilson is the embodiment of American culture-clash. As an African-American gay man, he is part of that so-called "intersection" of race and sexuality. When Wilson speaks of the need for African-American lesbians and gay men to "go home," the meaning is clear. But for a white-collar, middle-class, African-American gay man with AIDS, where is home located?

Improbable alliances challenge Wilson, who makes his home in several communities. He has shown a penchant for engaging disparate groups to address issues that each might not readily seek as its own. He once called for a people of color caucus "in the phone booth outside" at a major lesbian and gay conference. "This is a movement that still organizes out of people's personal phone books," he said. "People of color are unlisted."

But Wilson is noted for challenging fellow black gays and the African-American community at large with equal clarity. "We must remind families and friends every step of the way that some of us are gay and lesbian," he says, voicing one of his constant themes: *We need to go home.*

"The legacy of survival for the African-American people," says Wilson, "is our ability to support each other. That's what got us through slavery, that's what got us through Reconstruction, and that's what's going to get us through the hostility of the '90s and the 21st century."

Eric K. Washington

GOING HOME WITH THE VISIBLE MAN

PHOTO: Peter Ross

REAL WORLD HERO

PEDRO ZAMORA

Pedro Zamora's exemplary life ended back in Miami, where he died of AIDS in November 1994. Joining his family and friends in mourning were thousands of Americans who, through his personal activism and his uncompromising realness on *The Real World*, had come to appreciate his hard-won wisdom.

PHOTO: Ken Probst

Pedro Zamora's curious odyssey to fame began with the Mariel boatlift from Cuba in 1980, when he was eight years old. An honors student at Hialeah High School in Miami, Pedro was diagnosed with HIV in 1989, at age 17. His life seemed to be falling apart, until he volunteered to give a presentation about AIDS in his school. The trim, dark young man with the soulful eyes and the five-inch lashes was so effective and charismatic that a career in public service was born. Through organizations like Body Positive in Miami and Youth Empowerment Services (YES) in San Francisco, he flew all over the country to speak. In Iowa a newspaper picture of him holding a condom caused the local blood pressure to go through the roof.

On *The Real World*, in between games of pool, a relentless regimen of housework, and a burgeoning romance with his boyfriend Sean, Pedro was followed by the cameras to speaking engagements. He regularly fielded his housemates' questions about sex and HIV education. "I went public to use my story as leverage for people, to bring out their fears and get them talking," he tells them one evening, "to get them to think what they are putting at risk and what behavior they need to change." Though Pedro Zamora lived just twenty-two years, he affected a century's worth of lives.

Robert Rorke

SOMEONE'S ON THE FAIRWAY WITH DINAH

The Dinah Shore Golf Tournament is Dyke Heaven. Each March more than 5,000 lesbians pour into California's desert oasis for what has become the hottest ticket on the lesbian social calendar. With sunshine, golf, and girls, the tournament has become known as "the biggest dyke party west of the Mississippi."

Golf, of course, is secondary to many of Dinah's denizens. By early March, L.A.'s *Lesbian News* reaches fever pitch with its promotions for events featuring "luscious ladies." There is the Desert Palms Bra Party (guests are invited to wear their sexiest and most unusual bras) and an event called Le Moulin Rouge (which promises 3,000 très chic women), as well as the French Riviera Pool Party.

By Sunday the gals who gather at the Mission Hills clubhouse for beers are showing the strain of the sun, cruising, drinking, and golf. "It was girls as far as the eye could see," said my friend. For those few with energy left to burn, there was still the famous whipped cream wrestling night at Daddy Warbucks bar. I asked her if she'd go back next year. "In a heartbeat!"

Susan Reed

GREG LOUGANIS

the depth of a diver

GAMES WE PLAY

When it came to diving, Greg Louganis, eschewing standard role models, always had his own plan. "There was no one who could live up to what I wanted to achieve . . . I couldn't be afraid to leave everyone else behind—a fear most people feel," Louganis says. But in the rest of his life he felt different—an adopted, half-Samoan, dyslexic young man who was often called a sissy. "I had no expectations," he says. "As an adolescent, I never thought I would see my 30th birthday."

But at 35, the Olympic gold medalist made a move that once again left everyone behind. Rock Hudson, Arthur Ashe, Magic Johnson, and others revealed their HIV status to the world under pressure from the media or their illness. Louganis followed the inspiration of Ryan White, to whom his autobiography is dedicated. "I wanted to write my story, to have it reflect me and to maintain control."

"I don't want to set myself up to be a role model. There are facets of my life that people might be able to learn from," meaning the darker moments of depression, uncertainty, and the abuse he endured at the hands of his partner, all of which Louganis details in his book. "The scary part wasn't when I realized that I was lost. The scary part was when I didn't know that I was lost."

Greg Louganis is in many ways just starting to live.

Michael Goff

RUDY GALINDO: SOUL ON ICE

Rudy Galindo roared out of sporting oblivion to win the men's national title. Skating last in front of a sold-out audience of 10,869 at the San Jose Arena, Galindo—so little regarded that he hadn't even been included in the event's media guide—executed eight perfect triple jumps, including two difficult triple-triple combinations, to Tchaikovsky's *Swan Lake*. Even before he had finished his program, the electrified hometown crowd was on its feet. When the scores went up, seven of the nine judges had given Galindo first-place votes, enough to defeat his competitor.

The day after his San Jose victory, Galindo skated an exposition program to *Ave Maria* with a red AIDS ribbon pinned to his costume. During the past seven years, he has lost two coaches and an older brother to AIDS, and his father, Jess to a heart attack. "I skate for the people in my life, but also for the people who aren't here, for my coaches Jim [Hulick] and Rick [Inglesi], for my brother, George," says Galindo. "They're always with me on the ice. I call them the wind beneath my wings."

For Galindo, the greatest revelation about success has been that some things did not change. "For a little while I worried that I'd be walking down the street and someone would yell, 'Hey, there's Rudy Galindo! He's the gay skater. Let's go beat him up.'" Galindo has encountered nothing of the sort. Instead, he says, "The gay community has been great to me. The straight community has been great to me. All these straight men come up to me on the street and say, 'I watched your performance on TV, Rudy. You did it! And you made me cry.'"

Susan Reed

A GAY GAMES SCORECARD

Since 1982, when it was founded by Olympic athlete Tom Waddell, the Gay Games has become not only the world's premier lesbian and gay sporting event, but an opportunity for homosexuals everywhere to come together to celebrate what the body—and the mind—can do. Gay Games V is scheduled for 1998 in the Netherlands. It will be a massive event just like the 1994 Games, where there was strength in numbers.

Sporting events: **31**

Volunteers: **7,000**

Announcers: **52**

Countries represented: **40**

Drinking cups: **5,200**

Continents: **6**

Tennis balls: **6,000**

Languages: **20**

Shower towels: **75,000**

Dance parties: **20**

Cultural Festival exhibits/performances: **130**

St. Vincent Hospital physicians on call for people with HIV/AIDS: **7**

Hosts for housing: **250**

Requests for hosted housing: **1,000**

World records set at Gay Games: **1**

(in 100-meter butterfly, for age group 50-54, by Michael Mealiffe in 1990)

Funds committed by the Netherlands for Gay Games V in 1998: **$570,000**

Funds committed by the United States government for Gay Games IV: **$0**

Condoms from Mayer Labs for distribution on site: **250,000**

Bottles of pain-killers for distribution: **3,000**

WHAT CULTURE

DO WE MAKE

"Life is fabulous," RuPaul submits, dreamily, "I've hit pay dirt in terms of having real fun and tearing down walls around my heart." As far as his heart is concerned, we'll have to take his word for it, but as for his career, pay dirt is clearly an understatement. This erstwhile denizen of Atlanta's and New York's rather nasty drag scenes has risen to become, as he himself puts it, the "Queen of All Media." By cleaning up his notoriously ribald routines, he has dragged countless millions just a bit closer to the notion that difference does not equal danger.

He may be multitalented, but RuPaul's true gift lies in his king-size ambition. To those who wish he'd get back to his roots, he replies that he never left. "I just do what I do, just keep chug-a-luggin'.' If they like it, great, if not, OK." Indeed, his look may have evolved, but the message remains the same.

Ru muses about what his ever-increasing throngs of admirers should take away from his work as author, singer, dancer, actor, model, and finally, star. "I want the world to know that it's going to be all right. You can stop hating yourself. The party is just beginning."

Julian Fleisher

PHOTO: Albert Sanchez

THE FLIRTATIONS

On the Flirts' just released third album, aptly enti-
tled *Three* (Flirt)—their first without the late
Michael Callen—the trio bring it together with
"Everything Possible," their unofficial signature
song, a lullaby they wish they'd heard growing up.
"It's an amazing experience to be around people who
bring kids to our show," says Jon Arterton, who sings
in the group along with Jimmy Rutland.

Arterton continues, "When we first started traveling it
was a more intensely politicized time. It's always
interesting that except for the 10 largest cities,
it's everyone's perception that they live in an
area which is especially intolerant of gay people."

The newest member of the Flirtations is
honey-and-molasses-voiced Suede, a 15-year
music vet. "The surprise for me," she says of her
new gig, "has been that all of our community's talk
about celebrating diversity too often becomes about
identifying our similarities and not really embracing
our differences. Men and women are different and
it's a beautiful thing."

Andrew Velez

music

PLAY THAT COUNTRY MUSIC RIGHT, BOY

In 1991, after founding a gay country-western band, Doug Stevens called a New York weekly to lasso some media attention. The woman on the phone couldn't stop laughing. "Gays and lesbians," she said, "do not like country-western music." But as any veteran of a gay bar's two-step night could testify, country crooning—like the blues and disco—has always been near and dear to gay people's hearts, whether it's Patsy Cline's woes, Dolly Parton's campiness, or, well, Clint Black's Levi's. And now Stevens' The Outband and the duo Y'All are putting gay relationships at the heart of their music.

"I did everything I could to get away from the country culture," says Stevens, who moved from Mississippi to Missouri at 19. "I was abused by my father and blamed the culture for it." Still unsatisfied, he moved to New York in 1986—and broke into tears in a used-clothing store to the strains of Randy Travis.

"If we were heterosexual, we would be riding the wave," says Stevens, who has yet to play Nashville's Bluebird Cafe or sign a major label deal. "I'm not going to change who I am. That's why I have the band, because we're going to change the world."

"The music we do will never be played on country radio stations," says Y'All's Steven Cheslik-DeMeyer (right), the one who wears overalls. "It's closer to gospel and old-time string bands. We don't even really think of ourselves as country." Adds his partner Jay Byrd, the bald one in a dress, "We like to laugh."

Anderson Jones

PHOTO: Kim Hanson

83

THE REVEREND

PETER J. GOMES

THE WORD IS OUT

The first thing that strikes you is the voice. Mellifluous and refined, the accent is more Boston Brahmin than Baptist preacher. But then Peter J. Gomes is no ordinary clergyman. Minister at Harvard University's Memorial Church since 1974, this dignified, button-down gentleman seems perfectly at home amid the ivy and brick. Yet Harvard's Plummer Professor of Christian Morals—a Republican who took the podium at inaugural events for Ronald Reagan and George Bush—is also an out gay man.

Written like an extended homily, full of anecdote, wit and warmth, Gomes' book, *The Good Book*, argues that the Bible belongs to everyone—a living, dynamic document that means different things to different people. Gomes dismisses literal reading of the Bible as "dangerous and wrong." In perhaps the most engaging section of the book, "The Use and Abuse of the Bible," he takes a hard, close look at what the Bible really says about women, slavery, anti-Semitism, and, of course, homosexuality.

As for the place of gay men and lesbians in the Christian faith, Gomes is utterly confident. "The time is coming when spiritual questions will take center place, as opposed to discussions of rights and so forth," he forecasts of the gay movement. "And I want to be on the front lines when the spiritual turnaround happens."

Tom Beer

GEORGE WOLFE: RAGING WOLFE

As head of the New York Shakespeare Festival at the Public Theater, author of the breakaway hit *The Colored Museum*, and director of Tony Kushner's Pulitzer Prize-winning theatrical epic *Angels in America*, it's clear that George Wolfe sees theater as a vehicle for moving a social agenda. "I have to believe that," he says laughing. "I want to have an impact on the world, and theater is the only thing I'm good at." Besides, he claims, "theater transformed me, it empowered me at the moments in my life when I needed to be empowered, and I believe it's one of the places where community exists."

So how do we create social progress through the theater? "A series of fierce warriors from the various camps go forth—and wind up being clobbered," Wolfe says. "But in the process they change some people in power, who open the door just a little bit to let a few people in, and—once inside—they unlock the windows and let more people in. Racism only works if you surrender power to someone. When you embody your full power, people have to adjust. As a producer of this organization, one thing I'm trying to do is to create a truly American theater. And what is America? A whole bunch of energies colliding, all kinds of forces bouncing off one another and boundaries blurring. We are a nation of mutts. It's intrinsic to who we are, and that's what I want to put into the building."

Given how long it has taken to get homosexuality addressed meaningfully at all in the theater, it's a wonder so many gay people have stayed loyal to the stage. And while we waited, we've had to draw lessons for our lives from the heterosexual stories paraded in front of us, often written by gay men and lesbians. "Well," says George Wolfe with another grand gesture, "such is not the case at the Public Theater, let me tell you! Not anymore!"

Michael Lassell

CHERRY JONES: CHERRY'S JUBILEE

On the brink of major stardom, Cherry Jones has emerged as perhaps the only openly lesbian dramatic leading actress of our time. Throughout her stage career she has challenged the cloistered

PHOTO: Klaus Schoenwiese

hypocrisy that's practiced so prevalently in Hollywood—as she says, "I can't think of a time professionally when it seemed threatening to be out in the open about my sexuality."

Cherry Jones—she who bears her mother's maiden name as her first—grew up a free-spirited tomboy in Paris, Tennessee, with a strong affinity for the affections of women. She endured boundless crushes on her female schoolteachers and a tender longing for Julie Andrews. While at Carnegie Mellon in Pittsburgh, she had her first lesbian experience. "I was ever so grateful for it," she says, her intensely blue eyes as big as the wide Sapphic sea. "This seemed like the most natural, wonderful thing in the world. I was all set."

Cherry met her life-partner, architect Mary O'Connor, through mutual friends in January 1986. "Mary is truly an exceptional person," says Jones, her infatuation with her mate evident every time she mentions her name. "My family has all fallen so in love with Mary that I'm sure in my mother's religious mind it was divine inspiration that I was gay because she never would have known Mary."

A founding member of the American Repertory Theatre at Harvard, Jones has performed in 54 productions since 1978, ranging from Shakespeare to Tommy Tune's *Stepping Out*. She received a 1992 Tony nomination for her performance in *Our Country's Good* and won critical acclaim for her role in the 1994 production of Tennessee Williams' *Night of the Iguana*. The role that established her as a leading woman was as Catherine Sloper in *The Heiress*, for which she won the Tony.

Here is an actress whose gesture and disposition are the essential elements of her craft. "I have waited patiently for her star to rise," wrote columnist Liz Smith of the most talked-about leading lady of Broadway. "Her time is now."

Sue Carswell

READING SINCE THE REVOLUTION

For the twenty-fifth anniversary of Stonewall, we asked an assorted cast of cultural tastemakers—some writers, a few editors, and an outspoken drag queen—each to come up with five books published since 1969.

Blanche McCrary Boyd, author, *The Revolution of Little Girls*
Anything by Adrienne Rich
Odd Girls and *Twilight Lovers*, Lillian Faderman
Stone Butch Blues, Leslie Feinberg
States of Desire, Edmund White
A Thousand Acres, Jane Smiley

Dennis Cooper, author
Close to the Knives, David Wojnarowicz
Blood and Guts in High School, Kathy Acker
Prisoner of Love, Jean Genet
Draper, Larry Clark
The Compassion Protocol, Hervé Guibert

David B. Feinberg, author, *Queer and Loathing*
Dancer from the Dance, Andrew Holleran
Faggots, Larry Kramer
Metropolitan Life, Fran Lebowitz
The Irreversible Decline of Eddie Socket, John Weir
Tales of the City, Armistead Maupin

Richard Howard, poet, critic, translator

Poems and *A Wild Patience Has Taken Me This Far*, Adrienne Rich

Assumptions; *Presentation Piece*; *Separations*; and *Going Back to the River*, Marilyn Hacker

Selected Poems and *The Changing Light at Sandover*, James Merrill

Ode to Anna Moffo and Other Poems and *Rhapsodies of a Repeat Offender*, Wayne Koestenbaum

My Alexandria, Mark Doty

Kerry Fried, *New York Review of Books*

Animal Liberation (second edition, 1990), Peter Singer

Oranges Are Not the Only Fruit, Jeanette Winterson

The Fact of a Doorframe, Adrienne Rich

Against Forgetting: Twentieth-Century Poetry of Witness, Carolyn Forché, editor

Beginning With O, Olga Broumas, or *In a Time of Violence*, Eavan Boland

Larry Kramer, author

Christianity, Social Tolerance, and Homosexuality, John Boswell

Angels in America, Tony Kushner

Queer in America, Michelangelo Signorile

And the Band Played On, Randy Shilts

Being Homosexual, Dr. Richard Isay

B. Ruby Rich, critic

"Compulsory Heterosexuality and Lesbian Existence," essay, Adrienne Rich

"I Am Not a Woman," essay, Monique Wittig

"Only Women Stir My Imagination," essay, Blanche Wiesen Cook

Oranges Are Not the Only Fruit, Jeanette Winterson

Powers of Desire, Ann Snitow, Sharon Thompson, and Christine Stansell

RuPaul, singer, supermodel

A Return to Love, Marianne Williamson

Interview with the Vampire, Anne Rice

The Color Purple, Alice Walker

Secrets of a Sparrow, Diana Ross

Maybe the Moon, Armistead Maupin

Sapphire, poet and author

Zami, Audre Lorde

The Color Purple, Alice Walker

A Woman Is Talking to Death, Judy Grahn

In the Life, Joseph Beam, editor

Conditions: V, Barbara Smith and Lorraine Bethel, editors. (This volume of
  writing by black women contains the powerful poem "Where Will You Be?"
  by Pat Parker.)

Rose Troche, filmmaker

The Passion and *Written on the Body*, Jeanette Winterson

The Power of the Image, Annette Kuhn

Now You See It, Richard Dyer

How Do I Look?, Bad Object Choices, editors

Wide Angle, Vol. 14, No. 2 (special issue on gay and lesbian film), or *Skin Deep:
  Tales of Doomed Romance*, Charles Burns, or *Tongues of Flame*, David
  Wojnarowicz

Todd Oldham, fashion designer

I Was a White Slave in Harlem, Margo Howard-Howard ("After reading Margo
  Howard-Howard nothing else seems important.")

Sarah Pettit

HOW DO

WE LOVE

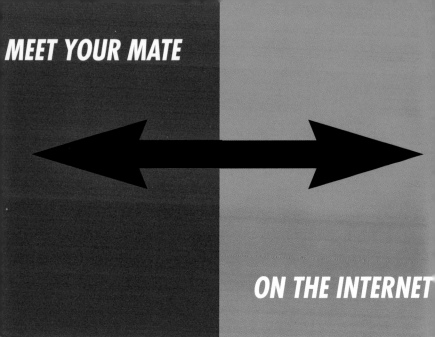

MEET YOUR MATE

ON THE INTERNET

CRUISING CYBERSPACE IN SEARCH OF MR. RIGHT

Queers have taken to cyberspace like it's going out of style. The cushion of anonymity that computer-message networking provides has made it easier, for example, to organize lesbian and gay groups in large corporations. Out on the infobahn, where no one ever has to know your real name and no one can show up with an ax at your E-mail address, it couldn't be easier to come out of the closet, discuss queer issues, organize, and meet new people, at least textually, and then, if you like what you read, arrange to meet in neutral territory.

The Internet has already spawned a slew of horror stories about people who misrepresent themselves on-line. It's best to keep your expectations low and your standards high when arranging a sight-unseen rendezvous. I've moved on from IRC and America Online to bulletin board services more specifically geared to electronic manhunting. My favorite service features almost exclusively local boys, individual profiles that can be called up before you even "chat" with someone, a match-making system, and an E-mail system. It's almost my Homo Shopping Club dream come true. Somewhere, floating in the tangled network of fiber-optic cables that circle the globe, there's a string of ASCII characters that may someday call itself my boyfriend. **James Hannaham**

WHAT TO CALL YOUR MATE

Once upon a time we had a language with connotations we understood, a language that fit our not-yet-ready-for-prime-time subcultural status. "Girlfriend" was what you had when you were first dating. "Lover" was what you graduated to, at least among lesbians, who heard in that word committed, domesticated, lively sexual affection. "My friend" was how we translated to the straight world, watching their eyes to see whether they looked nauseous when they understood. But now we've flung away our privacy—and language, as it is wont, lags behind.

So what words are we going to take up? We coupled queers face this dilemma almost daily. "Lover" of course is out; even among ourselves it's fading, probably because hearing it through het ears makes it sound salacious and temporary. And don't tell me "partner" is going to last. Every time I say it I feel as if I'm handling my love with asbestos gloves, antiseptically interpreting my life for the homo-impaired.

How about "spouse"? Recently, at a wedding, Marilyn and I sat next to two men who introduced each other to the straight folk as "my spouse Jerry" and "my spouse Myron." I nearly fell over in admiration. They explained that "spouse" accurately denotes their relationship, educating without putting people on guard. Unlike "partner," "spouse" at least puts the pair in the same bed; unlike "lover," "spouse" knows the bedroom is just one of many rooms in the house. And yet, greedy girl that I am, I'm not entirely satisfied with its chilly and bureaucratic past. Say we win in the Hawaii courts, and by some miracle other states acknowledge our Honolulu marriages. What will married queers call each other then?

Fortunately, the decision is not mine alone. Only 15 years ago, "spouse" would have invited the same snickers Jerry and Myron use it to deter. If Marilyn is not alone, if many mainstreamers are

PHOTO: David Armstrong. *Bruce and George in Paul's Bedroom, Providence*, 1977.
Courtesy of the artist and Matthew Marks Gallery, New York

waiting to occupy "husband" and "wife," our use of these words
might even change the world's view of marriage.

No, I don't honestly think I could say it yet, except as a joke;
"spouse" is still as far as I can go. Still, as a joke, it's coming out
of my mouth more and more often these days, and not just to
Marilyn and her laugh-track family. Once we trample the barriers
to marriage, I have a strange feeling many of us will use its termi-
nology seriously—with what results we'll soon discover.

So maybe what I'm saying comes down to this: Take my "wife."
Please.   **E. J. Graff**

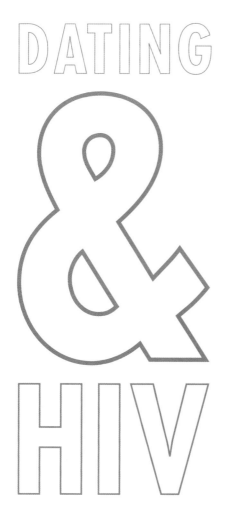

DATING & HIV

One day Ron walked off the plane and announced that he was HIV negative. I couldn't look him in the eye as I offered my congratulations. Our romance had hit a brick wall at 100 miles an hour, with no way to resolve the impasse. Was he the right one? Was he worth confirming my worst fears, quite possibly losing my mind in the process? I never found out, because I walked.

About a year later there was a coup d'etat in the State of Denial, and I was shipped into reality—or Siberia, as I now call it. I tested positive. Once you start dealing with AIDS, there is no turning back, because even if you don't tell anybody, even if you look "OK," the truth hangs over you. If you still want to continue the search for the perfect man—and face it, that's what most of us have built our lives on—then you're stuck on a roller coaster with no seat belt in sight.

In the past few years, as AIDS has become a mass reality, we've developed a new code, a subtle as well as obvious way to telegraph our status. Telling the truth about your status involves one's sense of self and the fear of loss—two key issues for gay men. "I wouldn't give you a blanket 'no' to dating HIV-positive men," says a negative friend, "but we need to face the fact that when two gay men are in a room alone, no matter what their status, there is a third person in the room. AIDS is kind of like adultery, an unspoken thing that neither party forgets, even if it's not discussed."

Being gay is like the *Odyssey*, a search for one's true self. Many of us spend years trying to be a person we're not. With self-recognition comes peace of mind. Then we want to share our great happiness with someone else, which is usually when the road gets bumpy. If it seems insurmountable, remember it has happened—even with the burden of HIV. It is happening right this very minute somewhere between two men who always said, "This can never happen to me."   **Kiki Mason**

THE FUTURE OF SAME-SEX MARRIAGE

The burgeoning marriage battle seems to prompt a subtle shift in how gay men and lesbians are being portrayed in America. Depictions of gay people as radical subversives, shower-room voyeurs, insubstantial party animals, and lonely AIDS victims are being replaced, or at least joined, by media portrayals of lesbians and gay men as devoted couples and just plain folks, in need of the same practical rights—tax status, immigration rights—as their straight counterparts. Conservatives who had never ceded an inch to the legitimacy of lesbian and gay relationships were suddenly arguing that while they resolutely opposed same-sex marriage, they certainly support the idea that gay couples should have hospital visitation or inheritance rights—not marriage, of course, but rights nonetheless.

PHOTO: Exum, Barney Frank (left) and Herb Moses

All this seemed to fly in the face of an old argument within the gay movement that the right to marriage is a political loser, and assimilationist to boot, and that gay people should fight for things like the Employment Non-Discrimination Act, hate-crime laws, and recognition of different kinds of family arrangements instead. After the adage that if you aim at the stars, you just might hit the moon, it was becoming apparent that all of those other issues were suddenly on the fast track precisely because same-sex marriage made them look moderate by comparison.

The battle for same-sex marriage is far from over, and victory is anything but assured. Indeed, the battle is only beginning. And because activists are trying to win same-sex marriage primarily in the courts rather than through public debate or in Congress and the state legislatures, the potential for backlash remains immense. With the possible outcomes veering between total acceptance of same-sex marriage on the one hand and a catastrophic Constitutional amendment forever banning it on the other, one thing is clear. We have seen a tectonic shift in the gay rights movement. From now on, love it or hate it, same-sex marriage is the main event.

Gabriel Rotello

HOLY MATRIMONY!

Since the dawn of time, the meaning of marriage has encompassed far more than can be included on the top tier of a wedding cake. The hidden history of marriage shows how gay men and lesbians can find the presence and the precedents they need to thrive.

1st century Rome: St. Paul calls marriage an inferior state to chastity. The historian Seutonius reports that emperor Nero married a man, Sporus, in an elaborate public ceremony.

4th century Rome: The empire passes a statute prohibiting same-sex marriages. Emperor Constantine Christianizes Roman marriage law.

1500s Spain: Under the Spanish Inquisition, marriage rights are denied to Jews and slaves. Elena de Cespedes, a Spanish woman who lived as a man and married a woman, is discovered and immolated.

1552 The Indies: Francisco López de Gómara's *History of the Indies* reports that in the New World, "the men marry other men who are impotent or castrated and go around like women."

1570s Rome: Montaigne reports that at the Church of St. John, Catholic priests perform same-sex marriages. A contemporary historian reports that same-sex couples married in St. John's are burned in the city square.

1576 Brazil: Spanish explorers report that some native women "give up all the duties of women and imitate men.... Each has a woman to serve her, to whom she says she is married, and they treat each other and speak with each other as man and wife."

19th–century Washington, D.C.: We'wha, a two-spirit leader and representative for the Native American Zuni tribe, is married to a man.

1901 New York: Mary Anderson dies; she lived as Murray Hall and married two women.

1930s Sudan: Anthropologists report among the Nuer tribe "a somewhat strange union ... in which a woman marries another woman and counts as the pater" of her children.

1947 California: As "Mr. and Mrs. David Warren," lesbian couple Thelma Jane Walker and Marieta Cook obtain a marriage license. An FBI investigation of the couple leads to charges of perjury.

1970 Minnesota: Richard Baker and James McConnell apply for a state marriage license, a request denied on May 22. The Minnesota Supreme Court, in *Baker vs. Nelson*, affirms the state's refusal the next year.

1973 Kentucky: The marriage license application of lesbian couple Tracy Knight and Marjorie Ruth Jones is denied as "the pursuit of hedonistic and sexual pleasure"; the Kentucky Supreme Court affirms the denial.

1974 Washington: The state Court of Appeals and Supreme Court affirm the state's refusal of same-sex marriage in *Singer vs. Hara*.

1974 Ohio: In Dayton, two black lesbian mothers on public assistance sue for the right to marry. They lack legal representation and gay community support, and their lawsuit fails.

1975 Colorado: In March, Clela Rorex, county clerk in Boulder, is approached by Dave Zamora and Ave McCord asking to be married. Not finding any laws prohibiting such a union, she marries them, and, eventually, five more same-sex couples. An irate cowboy shows up, demanding to be married to his horse, an eight-year-old mare. Rorex denies the union, saying that the horse is under age. The state attorney general advises Rorex against performing any more such unions.

1975 Maryland: In July, Montgomery County clerk's office issues a marriage license to Michelle Bush and Paulette Hall. A state attorney opines that the clerk cannot revoke the license once granted.

1982 Colorado: Two men—one a U.S. citizen, the other an alien—previously married by a county clerk and a minister, unsuccessfully petition the federal immigration service for the alien's reclassification.

1984 United States: The Unitarian Universalist Association votes to "affirm the growing practice of some of its ministers of conducting services of union of gay and lesbian couples."

1987 Denmark: The state enacts domestic partnership with most legal aspects of marriage except adoption. Norway follows suit in 1993; Sweden in 1995.

1991 Washington, D.C.: *Dean vs. D.C.* rules against plaintiffs Craig Dean and Patrick Gill, who sought to be married.

1993 United States: The General Assembly of the Union of American Hebrew Congregations adopts a resolution advocating legal recognition of same-sex unions.

1993 Hawaii: The state Supreme Court rules in *Baehr vs. Lewin* that denial of marriage licenses to same-sex couples is sex discrimination, and remands the case to trial court to allow the state to justify its case.

1996 Hawaii: A Hawaii judge declares that the state can legalize gay marriage.

Elise Harris

LOVE AND MARRIAGE

Throughout recorded history, same-sex couples have found ways
to tie the knot (or not) without official church or state sanction—
and, when necessary, to untie it and move on. And as some of us
seek the blessing of God, celebrate our unions before friends, or
even take on legal obligations, others are completely redefining
what it means to be together, or to be on their own. With no rules
dictated from above, we follow the dictates of our hearts.

So if—no, *when* we win the same right to marry that society
bestows upon straight people, it's still not likely gay men and lesbians will suddenly fall into step and march off to Levittown.
We're committed, all right: committed to leaving the private
details of our unions to the people involved.

Gay men and lesbians have brought relationships—and the single
life—into the '90s, and weddings are but one of many variations.
As the nation debates the legalization of gay marriage, we offer
these stories of gay and lesbian unions.

The Celebrities
"Once it's legal, we're first in line to get married," says Melissa
Etheridge, a force to be reckoned with in the usually boys-only

PHOTO: David Jensen, Julie Cypher (text) and Melissa Etheridge

world of guitar rock. "We are as committed spiritually and cere-moniously as a couple can be, and we are looking for the legal recognition that marriage gives." In the near decade since Etheridge and film and video director Julie Cypher met at the video shoot for Etheridge's "Bring Me Some Water," the two have had a private commitment ceremony, gotten matching thumb rings, and been showered with gifts from adoring fans. "When I'm on the road," says Etheridge, "people in the audience will shout, 'Hey, is Julie out there with you?' and it's kinda nice that there's an understanding that I have a life partner.

"There are a lot of benefits that marriage brings that people don't even consider," laments Etheridge. "I put a hot tub on the cabin we bought, and we end up paying taxes on it twice." These California girls agree that their wedding, if they were allowed one, would be outdoors. "And I think I would like it to be barefoot," Cypher says.

The Insiders
The closest thing to gay America's First Couple, Barney Frank, long-time Democratic congressman from Massachusetts, and Herb Moses, director of housing initiatives at federally chartered mort-gage lender Fannie Mae, don't worry about fitting into Washington, D.C.'s social and political milieu: they already do. "I have discussed our status as two men who live together in a

loving relationship on the floor of the U.S. House," says Frank.

Having met after Moses sent Frank a congratulatory note when the congressman first came out publicly in 1987, the two have been together ever since. While they both advocate same-sex marriage as a public policy issue, they don't see a need for it in their personal lives, nor for a commitment ceremony or rings (Moses says jewelry would be a liability in his work as a potter and Frank contends he would lose his down the drain). "Our lives are our ceremony and our commitment," says Frank. "I don't like the whole marriage discussion," says Moses. "Because people are saying, 'Well, you're not quite there,' and I think that Barney and I have been there for a long, long time."

The Independents

"My idea of a commitment ceremony is commiting Mark to Bellevue and my getting on a plane to St. Bart's," says fashion designer John Bartlett impishly of his longtime honey, Mark Welsh, a self-described "fledgling screenwriter." While Welsh typically refers to his beloved as his "significant tormentor," he has recently swapped that title for "owner-trainer-handler."

Although Welsh says they applaud and respect those working to legalize same-sex marriage, they're not about to bow down to that particular sacred cow. "Being gay is such an expression of individuality in itself, so marriage for me doesn't sit well," says Bartlett. Adds Welsh, "We've talked about [a commitment ceremony], if for no other reason than we can invite all of our heterosexual friends who we've spent millions of dollars on over the years as they've got married, divorced, married, divorced, and we can get, like, a new toaster."

The Widower

Five days after they met in November 1990, award-winning writer Paul Monette gave Winston Wilde a copy of Walt Whitman's *Leaves of Grass*, which he'd inscribed, "Welcome to the rest of our lives." "We were together four years, two months, and three weeks, and he died in my arms," says Wilde, from the house he shared with Monette in the Hollywood Hills, the house he now shares with his current "significant other," a boxer named Buddy. In April 1992, the couple had an impromptu wedding during a pagan ceremony, complete with serenade by Arlo Guthrie. Since Monette's death in February 1995, Wilde has lived a fairly cloistered existence. "I cherish my mourning Paul, and I'm not in a hurry to overcome it. For now this is my most profound form of intimacy with him. My public image is still as the widow Monette, but I don't want to be so dysfunctional. I want to get on with my life. I *am* on with my life."

The Entrepreneurs

In their professional lives and in their four-year relationship,
Angel Williams and Rebecca Walker share a serious sense of pur-
pose that only begins with the running of a coffee bar and cyber
lounge. "The idea behind Kokobar is to bring Internet access to
communities of color," says Williams. Kokobar is in Fort Greene,
Brooklyn, an urban, multicultural neighborhood. Walker, co-
founder of Third Wave, a young feminist activist group, and editor of the anthology *To Be Real* (Anchor), is upbeat about the
challenges of a dual romantic-professional partnership. "We've
found a way to really channel a lot of the love that we have for
each other into a kind of mutual support of these different
visions," she says.

Williams, a practicioner of Zen Buddhism, questions Walker's
focus on marriage's financial benefits and asserts that they already
have approval from the people who matter to them. "The affirma-
tion thing, that's great," says Williams, adding, "but I don't think
it has to be about that piece of paper." Walker finds common
ground. "The allure of marriage is for a kind of legitimacy and
stability," she says. "But the struggle to believe in oneself and to
be committed to love and the work of love is endless."

The Family

"Once I accepted that I wanted to be with men rather than

women, I didn't really expect to have children," says Lloyd Ziff, "so Stephen's children were like a really big blessing in my life." Ziff, a photographer, graphic designer, and art director, and Stephen Kelemen, an illustrator and painter, have been a family for nearly two decades, along with Chandra and her brother Pond.

For several years after the breakup of his 15-year marriage, Kelemen raised the children alone in rural Long Island. The two men and their dog, Tarzan, now split their time between that home and an apartment in Brooklyn. Neither has felt the need for marriage as a couple or as parents. Says Kelemen, "We maintain our relationship due to the fact that we make it up as we go along. There's a lot of individuality that I'd be afraid to give up and clamp something like marriage on it."

Ziff and Kelemen are also close to their two young grandsons, Pond's children. The kids call Ziff *zeyde*, Yiddish for "grandpa." "We introduced Pond to his wife, so I feel instrumental in their life," says Ziff. "So it's a very nice surprise."

Do they talk about growing old together? "We are growing old together," Ziff says, laughing.

Deb Schwartz

Tom Beer is managing editor of *Out* magazine. He has also written for *Poz*, *City Limits*, *QW*, and *LGNY*.

Susie Bright is a writer, activist, performer, and mother. She is the author and editor of twelve books, including *Susie Bright's Sexual State of the Union*.

Sue Carswell is a contributing writer to *Out* magazine and a senior editor at large at Pocket Books, where she has edited Lady Chablis' *Hiding My Candy* and Rudy Galindo's autobiography.

Kate Clinton is the oldest living American-born practicing lesbian comic in the continental United States.

Martin Duberman, distinguished professor of history at City University of New York, is the author of 17 books, most recently *A Queer World* and *Queer Representations*.

Heather Findlay is editor in chief of *Girlfriends*, a national lesbian magazine, and has been published widely in the popular and academic presses.

Julian Fleisher lives in the East Village of New York City. His latest book is *The Drag Queens of New York*.

Liz Galst won a 1994 National Lesbian and Gay Journalist Association Honors Award for her coverage of the Religious Right.

Michael Goff is the founder of *Out* magazine.

E.J. Graff's essays and fiction appear in such publications as *The New York Times*, *The Iowa Review*, *The Nation*, *The Village Voice*, and a variety of anthologies.

James Hannaham is a shady 'ho now appearing in glamazines like *Spin*, *Details*, *Us*, and the *New York Times Magazine*.

Elise Harris is news editor at *Out* magazine, and has written for *The Village Voice*, *The Nation*, and *Mademoiselle*.

Anderson Jones has just finished his own first book, *Men Together*, a collection of profiles of gay couples in long-term relationships.

Michael Lassell is features editor of *Metropolitan Home*, the author of a book of poetry, *The Hard Way*, and co-editor most recently of the anthology *Two Hearts Desire*.

Kiki Mason was a contributor to *Out* magazine, who died in 1995.

Ed Mickens is the author of *The 100 Best Companies for Gay Men and Lesbians*, and has moved home-base to Oakland, California.

Sara Miles is a contributing writer at *Out* magazine. She lives in San Francisco.

Michael Musto writes the weekly "La Dolce Musto" column in the *Village Voice* and is a correspondent on E's *Gossip Show*.

Sarah Pettit is co-founder and editor in chief of *Out* magazine.

Susan Reed is a senior editor at *Condé Nast Sports for Women* magazine in New York.

Ray Rogers is a contributing writer at *Out* magazine and music editor of *Interview*. He lives in New York with his husband, cats, birds, and bunny.

Robert Rorke is senior features editor at *Seventeen*. His articles have appeared in *New Woman*, *The Los Angeles Times*, *Brooklyn Bridge*, *Out* and other publications.

Gabriel Rotello, a former columnist for *New York Newsday*, is writing a book on the struggle for same-sex marriage. His book *Sexual Ecology* was published in 1997.

Deb Schwartz has written for *Spin*, the *Village Voice*, and *The Nation*. She is at work on a novel.

Bruce Shenitz lives in New York and writes and about legal affairs and social issues.

Alisa Solomon teaches at City University of New York, is a staff writer at the *Village Voice*, and is the author of the forthcoming *Re-Dressing the Canon: Essays on Theater and Gender*.

Andrew Velez is preparing a book about careers in American musical theater. An AIDS activist and founding member of Queer Nation, he is the father of two sons.

Eric K. Washington, who has written for *The New Yorker* and the *Village Voice*, received a first place award from the National Association of Black Journalists for "Going Home with the Visible Man," his profile of Phill Wilson.

BUTORS